Stray Birds

Stray Birds
by Rabindranath Tagore

A & D Publishing
PO Box 3005
Radford VA 24143-3005
www.wilderpublications.com

ISBN 10: 1-60459-533-7
ISBN 13: 978-1-60459-533-8

First Edition

1

Stray birds of summer come to my window to sing and fly away. And yellow leaves of autumn, which have no songs, flutter and fall there with a sigh.

2

O troupe of little vagrants of the world, leave your footprints in my words.

3

The world puts off its mask of vastness to its lover. It becomes small as one song, as one kiss of the eternal.

4

It is the tears of the earth that keep her smiles in bloom.

5

The mighty desert is burning for the love of a blade of grass who shakes her head and laughs and flies away.

6

If you shed tears when you miss the sun, you also miss the stars.

7

The sands in your way beg for your song and your movement, dancing water. Will you carry the burden of their lameness?

8

Her wistful face haunts my dreams like the rain at night.

9

Once we dreamt that we were strangers. We wake up to find that we were dear to each other.

10

Sorrow is hushed into peace in my heart like the evening among the silent trees.

11

Some unseen fingers, like idle breeze, are playing upon my heart the music of the ripples.

12

"What language is thine, O sea?"

"The language of eternal question."

"What language is thy answer, O sky?

"The language of eternal silence."

13

Listen, my heart, to the whispers of the world with which it makes love to you.

14

The mystery of creation is like the darkness of night—it is great. Delusions of knowledge are like the fog of the morning.

15

Do not seat your love upon a precipice because it is high.

16

I sit at my window this morning where the world like a passer-by stops for a moment, nods to me and goes.

17

These little thoughts are the rustle of leaves; they have their whisper of joy in my mind.

18

What you are you do not see, what you see is your shadow.

19

My wishes are fools, they shout across thy songs, my Master. Let me but listen.

20

I cannot choose the best.

The best chooses me.

21

They throw their shadows before them who carry their lantern on their back.

22

That I exist is a perpetual surprise which is life.

23

"We, the rustling leaves, have a voice that answers the storms, but who are you so silent?" "I am a mere flower."

24

Rest belongs to the work as the eyelids to the eyes.

25

Man is a born child, his power is the power of growth.

26

God expects answers for the flowers he sends us, not for the sun and the earth.

27

The light that plays, like a naked child, among the green leaves happily knows not that man can lie.

28

O Beauty, find thyself in love, not in the flattery of thy mirror.

29

My heart beats her waves at the shore of the world and writes upon it her signature in tears with the words, "I love thee."

30

"Moon, for what do you wait?"

"To salute the sun for whom I must make way."

31

The trees come up to my window like the yearning voice of the dumb earth.

32

His own mornings are new surprises to God.

33

Life finds its wealth by the claims of the world, and its worth by the claims of love.

34

The dry river-bed finds no thanks for its past.

35

The bird wishes it were a cloud. The cloud wishes it were a bird.

36

The waterfall sings, "I find my song, when I find my freedom."

37

I cannot tell why this heart languishes in silence.

It is for small needs it never asks, or knows or remembers.

38

Woman, when you move about in your household service your limbs sing like a hill stream among its pebbles.

39

The sun goes to cross the Western sea, leaving its last salutation to the East.

40

Do not blame your food because you have no appetite.

41

The trees, like the longings of the earth, stand a-tiptoe to peep at the heaven.

42

You smiled and talked to me of nothing and I felt that for this I had been waiting long.

43

The fish in the water is silent, the animal on the earth is noisy, the bird in the air is singing,

But Man has in him the silence of the sea, the noise of the earth and the music of the air.

44

The world rushes on over the strings of the lingering heart making the music of sadness.

45

He has made his weapons his gods. When his weapons win he is defeated himself.

46

God finds himself by creating.

47

Shadow, with her veil drawn, follows Light in secret meekness, with her silent steps of love.

48

The stars are not afraid to appear like fireflies.

49

I thank thee that I am none of the wheels of power but I am one with the living creatures that are crushed by it.

50

The mind, sharp but not broad, sticks at every point but does not move.

51

Your idol is shattered in the dust to prove that God's dust is greater than your idol.

52

Man does not reveal himself in his history, he struggles up through it.

53

While the glass lamp rebukes the earthen for calling it cousin, the moon rises, and the glass lamp, with a bland smile, calls her, "My dear, dear sister."

54

Like the meeting of the seagulls and the waves we meet and come near.
The seagulls fly off, the waves roll away and we depart.

55

My day is done, and I am like a boat drawn on the beach, listening to
the dance-music of the tide in the evening.

56

Life is given to us, we earn it by giving it.

57

We come nearest to the great when we are great in humility.

58

The sparrow is sorry for the peacock at the burden of its tail.

59

Never be afraid of the moments—thus sings the voice of the everlasting.

60

The hurricane seeks the shortest road by the no-road, and suddenly
ends its search in the Nowhere.

61

Take my wine in my own cup, friend. It loses its wreath of foam when poured into that of others.

62

The Perfect decks itself in beauty for the love of the Imperfect.

63

God says to man, "I heal you therefore I hurt, love you therefore punish."

64

Thank the flame for its light, but do not forget the lampholder standing in the shade with constancy of patience.

65

Tiny grass, your steps are small, but you possess the earth under your tread.

66

The infant flower opens its bud and cries, "Dear World, please do not fade."

67

God grows weary of great kingdoms, but never of little flowers.

68

Wrong cannot afford defeat but Right can.

69

"I give my whole water in joy," sings the waterfall, "though little of it is enough for the thirsty."

70

Where is the fountain that throws up these flowers in a ceaseless outbreak of ecstasy?

71

The woodcutter's axe begged for its handle from the tree. The tree gave it.

72

In my solitude of heart I feel the sigh of this widowed evening veiled with mist and rain.

73

Chastity is a wealth that comes from abundance of love.

74

The mist, like love, plays upon the heart of the hills and brings out surprises of beauty.

75

We read the world wrong and say that it deceives us.

76

The poet wind is out over the sea and the forest to seek his own voice.

77

Every child comes with the message that God is not yet discouraged of man.

78

The grass seeks her crowd in the earth.

The tree seeks his solitude of the sky.

79

Man barricades against himself.

80

Your voice, my friend, wanders in my heart, like the muffled sound of the sea among these listening pines.

81

What is this unseen flame of darkness whose sparks are the stars?

82

Let life be beautiful like summer flowers and death like autumn leaves.

88

He who wants to do good knocks at the gate; he who loves finds the gate open.

84

In death the many becomes one; in life the one becomes many. Religion will be one when God is dead.

85

The artist is the lover of Nature, therefore he is her slave and her master.

86

"How far are you from me, O Fruit?" "I am hidden in your heart, O Flower."

87

This longing is for the one who is felt in the dark, but not seen in the day.

88

"You are the big drop of dew under the lotus leaf, I am the smaller one on its upper side," said the dewdrop to the lake.

89

The scabbard is content to be dull when it protects the keenness of the sword.

90

In darkness the One appears as uniform; in the light the One appears as manifold.

91

The great earth makes herself hospitable with the help of the grass.

92

The birth and death of the leaves are the rapid whirls of the eddy whose wider circles move slowly among stars.

93

Power said to the world, "You are mine. The world kept it prisoner on her throne. Love said to the world, "I am thine." The world gave it the freedom of her house.

94

The mist is like the earth's desire. It hides the sun for whom she cries.

95

Be still, my heart, these great trees are prayers.

96

The noise of the moment scoffs at the music of the Eternal.

97

I think of other ages that floated upon the stream of life and love and death and are forgotten, and I feel the freedom of passing away.

98

The sadness of my soul is her bride's veil. It waits to be lifted in the night.

99

Death's stamp gives value to the coin of life; making it possible to buy with life what is truly precious.

100

The cloud stood humbly in a corner of the sky. The morning crowned it with splendour.

101

The dust receives insult and in return offers her flowers.

102

Do not linger to gather flowers to keep them, but walk on, for flowers will keep themselves blooming all your way.

103

Roots are the branches down in the earth. Branches are roots in the air.

104

The music of the far-away summer flutters around the Autumn seeking its former nest.

105

Do not insult your friend by lending him merits from your own pocket.

106

The touch of the nameless days clings to my heart like mosses round the old tree.

107

The echo mocks her origin to prove she is the original.

108

God is ashamed when the prosperous boasts of His special favour.

109

I cast my own shadow upon my path, because I have a lamp that has not been lighted.

110

Man goes into the noisy crowd to drown his own clamour of silence.

111

That which ends in exhaustion is death, but the perfect ending is in the endless.

112

The sun has his simple robe of light. The clouds are decked with gorgeousness.

113

The hills are like shouts of children who raise their arms, trying to catch stars.

114

The road is lonely in its crowd for it is not loved.

115

The power that boasts of its mischiefs is laughed at by the yellow leaves that fall, and clouds that pass by.

116

The earth hums to me to-day in the sun, like a woman at her spinng, some ballad of the ancient time in a forgotten tongue.

117

The grass-blade is worth of the great world where it grows.

118

Dream is a wife who must talk.

Sleep is a husband who silently suffers.

119

The night kisses the fading day whispering to his ear, "I am death, your mother. I am to give you fresh birth."

120

I feel, thy beauty, dark night, like that of the loved woman when she has put out the lamp.

121

I carry in my world that flourishes the worlds that have failed.

122

Dear friend, I feel the silence of your great thoughts of may a deepening eventide on this beach when I listen to these waves.

123

The bird thinks it is an act of kindness to give the fish a lift in the air.

124

"In the moon thou sendest thy love letters to me," said the night to the sun.

"I leave my answers in tears upon the grass."

125

The Great is a born child; when he dies he gives his great childhood to the world.

126

Not hammerstrokes, but dance of the water sings the pebbles into perfection.

127

Bees sip honey from flowers and hum their thanks when they leave.

The gaudy butterfly is sure that the flowers owe thanks to him.

128

To be outspoken is easy when you do not wait to speak the complete truth.

129

Asks the Possible to the Impossible, "Where is your dwelling place?"

"In the dreams of the impotent," comes the answer.

130

If you shut your door to all errors truth will be shut out.

131

I hear some rustle of things behind my sadness of heart,—I cannot see them.

132

Leisure in its activity is work.

The stillness of the sea stirs in waves.

133

The leaf becomes flower when it loves.

The flower becomes fruit when it worships.

134

The roots below the earth claim no rewards for making the branches fruitful.

135

This rainy evening the wind is restless.

I look at the swaying branches and ponder over the greatness of all things.

136

Storm of midnight, like a giant child awakened in the untimely dark, has begun to play and shout.

137

Thou raisest thy waves vainly to follow thy lover. O sea, thou lonely bride of the storm.

138

"I am ashamed of my emptiness," said the Word to the Work.

"I know how poor I am when I see you," said the Work to the Word.

139

Time is the wealth of change, but the clock in its parody makes it mere change and no wealth.

140

Truth in her dress finds facts too tight.

In fiction she moves with ease.

141

When I travelled to here and to there, I was tired of thee, O Road, but now when thou leadest me to everywhere I am wedded to thee in love.

142

Let me think that there is one among those stars that guides my life through the dark unknown.

143

Woman, with the grace of your fingers you touched my things and order came out like music.

144

One sad voice has its nest among the ruins of the years. It sings to me in the night,—"I loved you."

145

The flaming fire warns me off by its own glow.

Save me from the dying embers hidden under ashes.

146

I have my stars in the sky,

But oh for my little lamp unlit in my house.

147

The dust of the dead words clings to thee.

Wash thy soul with silence.

148

Gaps are left in life through which comes the sad music of death.

149

The world has opened its heart of light in the morning.

Come out, my heart, with thy love to meet it.

150

My thoughts shimmer with these shimmering leaves and my heart sings with the touch of this sunlight; my life is glad to be floating with all things into the blue of space, into the dark of time.

151

God's great power is in the gentle breeze, not in the storm.

152

This is a dream in which things are all loose and they oppress.

I shall find them gathered in thee when I awake and shall be free.

153

"Who is there to take up my duties?" asked the setting sun.

"I shall do what I can, my Master," said the earthen lamp.

154

By plucking her petals you do not gather the beauty of the flower.

155

Silence will carry your voice like the nest that holds the sleeping birds.

156

The Great walks with the Small without fear.

The Middling keeps aloof.

157

The night opens the flowers in secret and allows the day to get thanks.

158

Power takes as ingratitude the writhings of its victims.

159

When we rejoice in our fulness, then we can part with our fruits with joy.

160

The raindrops kissed the earth and whispered,—"We are thy homesick children, mother, come back to thee from the heaven."

161

The cobweb pretends to catch dew-drops and catches flies.

162

Love! when you come with the burning lamp of pain in your hand, I can see your face and know you as bliss.

163

"The learned say that your lights will one day be no more." said the firefly to the stars. The stars made no answer.

164

In the dusk of the evening the bird of some early dawn comes to the nest of my silence.

165

Thoughts pass in my mind like flocks of ducks in the sky.

I hear the voice of their wings.

166

The canal loves to think that rivers exist solely to supply it with water.

167

The world has kissed my soul with its pain, asking for its return in songs.

168

That which oppresses me, is it my soul trying to come out in the open, or the soul of the world knocking at my heart for its entrance?

169

Thought feeds itself with its own words and grows.

170

I have dipped the vessel of my heart into this silent hour; it has filled with love.

171

Either you have work or you have not.

When you have to say, "Let us do something," then begins mischief.

172

The sunflower blushed to own the nameless flower as her kin.

The sun rose and smiled on it, saying, "Are you well, my darling?"

173

"Who drives me forward like fate?" "The Myself striding on my back."

174

The clouds fill the watercups of the river, hiding themselves in the distant hills.

175

I spill water from my water jar as I walk on my way,

Very little remains for my home.

176

The water in a vessel is sparkling; the water in the sea is dark.

The small truth has words that are clear; the great truth has great silence.

177

Your smile was the flowers of your own fields, your talk was the rustle of your own mountain pines, but your heart was the woman that we all know.

178

It is the little things that I leave behind for my loved ones,— great things are for everyone.

179

Woman, thou hast encircled the world's heart with the depth of thy tears as the sea has the earth.

180

The sunshine greets me with a smile. The rain, his sad sister, talks to my heart.

181

My flower of the day dropped its petals forgotten. In the evening it ripens into a golden fruit of memory.

182

I am like the road in the night listening to the footfalls of its memories in silence.

183

The evening sky to me is like a window, and a lighted lamp, and a waiting behind it.

184

He who is too busy doing good finds no time to be good.

185

I am the autumn cloud, empty of rain, see my fulness in the field of ripened rice.

186

They hated and killed and men praised them.

But God in shame hastens to hide its memory under the green grass.

187

Toes are the fingers that have forsaken their past.

188

Darkness travels towards light, but blindness towards death.

189

The pet dog suspects the universe for scheming to take its place.

190

Sit still my heart, do not raise your dust.

Let the world find its way to you.

191

The bow whispers to the arrow before it speeds forth—"Your freedom is mine."

192

Woman, in your laughter you have the music of the fountain of life.

193

A mind all logic is like a knife all blade.

It makes the hand bleed that uses it.

194

God loves man's lamp lights better than his own great stars.

195

This world is the world of wild storms kept tame with the music of beauty.

196

"My heart is like the golden casket of thy kiss," said the sunset cloud to the sun.

197

By touching you may kill, by keeping away you may possess.

198

The cricket's chirp and the patter of rain come to me through the dark, like the rustle of dreams from my past youth.

199

"I have lost my dewdrop," cries the flower to the morning sky that has lost all its stars.

200

The burning log bursts in flame and cries,—"This is my flower, my death."

201

The wasp thinks that the honey-hive of the neighbouring bees is too small.

His neighbours ask him to build one still smaller.

202

"I cannot keep your waves," says the bank to the river. "Let me keep your footprints in my heart."

203

The day, with the noise of this little earth, drowns the silence of all worlds.

204

The song feels the infinite in the air, the picture in the earth,

the poem in the air and the earth;

For its words have meaning that walks and music that soars.

205

When the sun goes down to the West, the East of his morning stands before him in silence.

206

Let me not put myself wrongly to my world and set it against me.

207

Praise shames me, for I secretly beg for it.

208

Let my doing nothing when I have nothing to do become untroubled in its depth of peace like the evening in the seashore when the water is silent.

209

Maiden, your simplicity, like the blueness of the lake, reveals your depth of truth.

210

The best does not come alone. It comes with the company of the all.

211

God's right hand is gentle, but terrible is his left hand.

212

My evening came among the alien trees and spoke in a language which my morning stars did not know.

213

Night's darkness is a bag that bursts with the gold of the dawn.

214

Our desire lends the colours of the rainbow to the mere mists and vapours of life.

215

God waits to win back his own flowers as gifts from man's hands.

216

My sad thoughts tease me asking me their own names.

217

The service of the fruit is precious, the service of the flower is sweet, but let my service be the service of the leaves in its shade of humble devotion.

218

My heart has spread its sails to the idle winds for the shadowy island of Anywhere.

219

Men are cruel, but Man is kind.

220

Make me thy cup and let my fulness be for thee and for thine.

221

The storm is like the cry of some god in pain whose love the earth refuses.

222

The world does not leak because death is not a crack.

223

Life has become richer by the love that has been lost.

224

My friend, your great heart shone with the sunrise of the East like the snowy summit of a lonely hill in the dawn.

225

The fountain of death makes the still water of life play.

226

Those who have everything but thee, my God, laugh at those who have nothing but thyself.

227

The movement of life has its rest in its own music.

228

Kicks only raise dust and not crops from the earth.

229

Our names are the light that glows on the sea waves at night and then dies without leaving its signature.

230

Let him only see the thorns who has eyes to see the rose.

231

Set bird's wings with gold and it will never again soar in the sky.

232

The same lotus of our clime blooms here in the alien water with the same sweetness, under another name.

233

In heart's perspective the distance looms large.

234

The moon has her light all over the sky, her dark spots to herself.

235

Do not say, "It is morning," and dismiss it with a name of yesterday. See it for the first time as a new-born child that has no name.

236

Smoke boasts to the sky, and Ashes to the earth, that they are brothers to the fire.

237

The raindrop whispered to the jasmine, "Keep me in your heart for ever." The jasmine sighed, "Alas," and dropped to the ground.

238

Timid thoughts, do not be afraid of me.

I am a poet.

239

The dim silence of my mind seems filled with crickets' chirp—the grey twilight of sound.

240

Rockets, your insult to the stars follows yourself back to the earth.

241

Thou hast led me through my crowded travels of the day to my evening's loneliness.

I wait for its meaning through the stillness of the night.

242

This life is the crossing of a sea, where we meet in the same narrow ship.

In death we reach the shore and go to our different worlds.

243

The stream of truth flows through its channels of mistakes.

244

My heart is homesick to-day for the one sweet hour across the sea of time.

245

The bird-song is the echo of the morning light back from the earth.

246

"Are you too proud to kiss me?" the morning light asks the buttercup.

247

"How may I sing to thee and worship, O Sun?" asked the little flower.

"By the simple silence of thy purity," answered the sun.

248

Man is worse than an animal when he is an animal.

249

Dark clouds become heaven's flowers when kissed by light.

250

Let not the sword-blade mock its handle for being blunt.

251

The night's silence, like a deep lamp, is burning with the light of its milky way.

252

Around the sunny island of Life swells day and night death's limitless song of the sea.

253

Is not this mountain like a flower, with its petals of hills, drinking the sunlight?

254

The real with its meaning read wrong and emphasis misplaced is the unreal.

255

Find your beauty, my heart, from the world's movement, like the boat that has the grace of the wind and the water.

256

The eyes are not proud of their sight but of their eyeglasses.

257

I live in this little world of mine and am afraid to make it the least less. Lift me into thy world and let me have the freedom gladly to lose my all.

258

The false can never grow into truth by growing in power.

259

My heart, with its lapping waves of song, longs to caress this green world of the sunny day.

260

Wayside grass, love the star, then your dreams will come out in flowers.

261

Let your music, like a sword, pierce the noise of the market to its heart.

262

The trembling leaves of this tree touch my heart like the fingers of an infant child.

263

This sadness of my soul is her bride's veil.

It waits to be lifted in the night.

264

The little flower lies in the dust. It sought the path of the butterfly.

265

I am in the world of the roads. The night comes. Open thy gate, thou world of the home.

266

I have sung the songs of thy day. In the evening let me carry thy lamp through the stormy path.

267

I do not ask thee into the house. Come into my infinite loneliness, my Lover.

268

Death belongs to life as birth does. The walk is in the raising of the foot as in the laying of it down.

269

I have learnt the simple meaning of thy whispers in flowers and sunshine—teach me to know thy words in pain and death.

270

The night's flower was late when the morning kissed her, she shivered and sighed and dropped to the ground.

271

Through the sadness of all things I hear the crooning of the Eternal Mother.

272

I came to your shore as a stranger, I lived in your house as a guest, I leave your door as a friend, my earth.

273

Let my thoughts come to you, when I am gone, like the afterglow of sunset at the margin of starry silence.

274

Light in my heart the evening star of rest and then let the night whisper to me of love.

275

I am a child in the dark.

I stretch my hands through the coverlet of night for thee, Mother.

276

The day of work is done. Hide my face in your arms, Mother. Let me dream.

277

The lamp of meeting burns long; it goes out in a moment at the parting.

278

One word keep for me in thy silence, O World, when I am dead, "I have loved."

279

We live in this world when we love it.

280

Let the dead have the immortality of fame, but the living the immortality of love.

281

I have seen thee as the half-awakened child sees his mother in the dusk of the dawn and then smiles and sleeps again.

282

I shall die again and again to know that life is inexhaustible.

283

While I was passing with the crowd in the road I saw thy smile from the balcony and I sang and forgot all noise.

284

Love is life in its fulness like the cup with its wine.

285

They light their own lamps and sing their own words in their temples.

But the birds sing thy name in thine own morning light,—for thy name is joy.

286

Lead me in the centre of thy silence to fill my heart with songs.

287

Let them live who choose in their own hissing world of fireworks.

My heart longs for thy stars, my God.

288

Love's pain sang round my life like the unplumbed sea, and love's joy sang like birds in its flowering groves.

289

Put out the lamp when thou wishest.

I shall know thy darkness and shall love it.

290

When I stand before thee at the day's end thou shalt see my scars and know that I had my wounds and also my healing.

291

Some day I shall sing to thee in the sunrise of some other world,

"I have seen thee before in the light of the earth, in the love of man."

292

Clouds come floating into my life from other days no longer to shed rain or usher storm but to give colour to my sunset sky.

293

Truth raises against itself the storm that scatters its seeds broadcast.

294

The storm of the last night has crowned this morning with golden peace.

295

Truth seems to come with its final word; and the final word gives birth to its next.

296

Blessed is he whose fame does not outshine his truth.

297

Sweetness of thy name fills my heart when I forget mine—like thy morning sun when the mist is melted.

298

The silent night has the beauty of the mother and the clamorous day of the child.

299

The world loved man when he smiled. The world became afraid of him when he laughed.

300

God waits for man to regain his childhood in wisdom.

301

Let me feel this world as thy love taking form, then my love will help it.

302

Thy sunshine smiles upon the winter days of my heart, never doubting of its spring flowers.

303

God kisses the finite in his love and man the infinite.

304

Thou crossest desert lands of barren years to reach the moment of fulfilment.

305

God's silence ripens man's thoughts into speech.

306

Thou wilt find, Eternal Traveller, marks of thy footsteps across my songs.

307

Let me not shame thee, Father, who displayest thy glory in thy children.

308

Cheerless is the day, the light under frowning clouds is like a punished child with traces of tears on its pale cheeks, and the cry of the wind is like the cry of a wounded world. But I know I am travelling to meet my Friend.

309

To-night there is a stir among the palm leaves, a swell in the sea, Full Moon, like the heart throb of the world. From what unknown sky hast thou carried in thy silence the aching secret of love?

310

I dream of a star, an island of light, where I shall be born and in the depth of its quickening leisure my life will ripen its works like the ricefield in the autumn sun.

311

The smell of the wet earth in the rain rises like a great chant of praise from the voiceless multitude of the insignificant.

312

That love can ever lose is a fact that we cannot accept as truth.

313

We shall know some day that death can never rob us of that which our soul has gained, for her gains are one with herself.

314

God comes to me in the dusk of my evening with the flowers from my past kept fresh in his basket.

315

When all the strings of my life will be tuned, my Master, then at every touch of thine will come out the music of love.

316

Let me live truly, my Lord, so that death to me become true.

317

Man's history is waiting in patience for the triumph of the insulted man.

318

I feel thy gaze upon my heart this moment like the sunny silence of the morning upon the lonely field whose harvest is over.

319

I long for the Island of Songs across this heaving Sea of Shouts.

320

The prelude of the night is commenced in the music of the sunset, in its solemn hymn to the ineffable dark.

321

I have scaled the peak and found no shelter in fame's bleak and barren height. Lead me, my Guide, before the light fades, into the valley of quiet where life's harvest mellows into golden wisdom.

322

Things look phantastic in this dimness of the dusk—the spires whose bases are lost in the dark and tree tops like blots of ink. I shall wait for the morning and wake up to see thy city in the light.

323

I have suffered and despaired and known death and I am glad that I am in this great world.

324

There are tracts in my life that are bare and silent. They are the open spaces where my busy days had their light and air.

325

Release me from my unfulfilled past clinging to me from behind making death difficult.

326

Let this be my last word, that I trust in thy love.